The Sayings of Winston Churchill

The Sayings of

WINSTON
CHURCHILL

edited by

J.A. SUTCLIFFE

with an introduction by

ROBERT BLAKE

Duckworth

Second impression 1992
First published in 1992 by
Gerald Duckworth & Co. Ltd.
The Old Piano Factory
48 Hoxton Square, London N1 6PB
Tel: 071 729 5986
Fax: 071 729 0015

A catalogue record for this book is available
from the British Library

ISBN 0 7156 2389 3

Typeset by Ray Davies
Printed in Great Britain by
Redwood Press Limited, Melksham

Contents

Sources

Works by Churchill

Great Contemporaries (1937)
History of the English-Speaking Peoples (4 vols, 1956-58)
Lord Randolph Churchill (1906)
The Malakand Field Force (1898)
My Early Life (1930)
The People's Rights (1909)
The River War (1899)
Savrola (1900)
The Second World War (6 vols, 1948-54)
Thoughts and Adventures (1932)
While England Slept (1936)
The World Crisis (5 vols, 1923-31)

Other sources

Maurice Ashley, *Churchill as Historian* (1968)
D. Bardens, *Churchill in Parliament* (1967)
Violet Bonham-Carter, *Winston Churchill As I Knew Him* (1965)
Piers Brendon, *Winston Churchill: A Brief Life* (1984)
L. Broad, *Winston Churchill* (1956)
Sarah Churchill, *A Thread in the Tapestry* (1967)
John Colville, *The Fringes of Power* (1985)
Guy Eden, *Portrait of Churchill* (1945)
Sir Peter Gretton, *Former Naval Person* (1968)
Sir Ernest Gowers, *Plain Words* (1948)
Harold Macmillan, *The Blast of War* (1967)
W. Manchester, *The Caged Lion* (1988)
J. Marchant (ed.), *Winston Spencer Churchill: Servant of Crown and Commonwealth* (1954)
Nigel Nicholson (ed.), *Harold Nicholson, Diaries and Letters 1939-1945* (1967)
E.T. Raymond, *Mr Balfour* (1920)
Peter Stansky (ed.) *Churchill: A Profile* (1973)
Hugh Thomas, *The Suez Affair* (1967)

Introduction

by Robert Blake

Only two British Prime Ministers have been
'professional' writers, if one can use the adjective in the
sense of spending a large part of their lives writing for
money. The first was Benjamin Disraeli, the second
Winston Churchill (1874-1965). Their genres were
different. Disraeli was a novelist who also wrote one
biography. Churchill was a biographer and historian
who also wrote one novel. Each had a command of
language and an idiosyncratic style which cannot be
confused with that of anyone else. Who but Disraeli
could describe a basket of prawns as 'the rosy coloured
tribute of Torbay'? Who but Churchill could refer to a
tall, humourless minister as 'that Wuthering Height'?
They were masters of both the spoken and the written
word, and their memorable epigrams, phrases and
witticisms are to be found as much in their speeches as
in their writings.

Churchill evinced his love of words at an early stage.
He may have derived it from his father whom he
worshipped but who regarded him as a dolt and put
him into the Army for that reason. Lord Randolph,
second son of the seventh Duke of Marlborough, was a
master of invective. His description of Gladstone as 'an
old man in a hurry' has echoed down the years. A
potentially brilliant political career was cut short by an
impetuous resignation. He died of a brain disease eight
years later in January 1895. Winston's relations with his
American mother were no easier than with his father.
She was extravagant, and so was he. There was no
money. An impecunious subaltern bent on emulating his
father in politics had to earn enough for independence.
The only way was by his pen. Something of his flair for
words had been shown by his winning the Declamation
Prize at Harrow by reciting 1,200 lines of Macaulay's

Lays of Ancient Rome. His memory, long into old age, remained astonishing. He later came to hate Macaulay for traducing the great Duke John, his ancestor, but in his youth Macaulay's *History* and *Essays* along with Gibbon's *Decline and Fall* were paramount influences on his style.

Deftly pulling every string he could, he managed to combine soldiering with journalism as a war correspondent, and turned his articles into profitable books. These, together with lucrative American lectures, enabled him to accumulate some £10,000 (at least £250,000 in modern values) before resigning from the Army and winning a seat as a Conservative in 1900, just after his sensational escape as a prisoner of war of the Boers. That episode together with his crossing the floor of the House in 1904 made him a celebrity, though detested by the Conservatives and not much trusted by his new party. But he became a Liberal minister in 1906, publishing in the same year his life of his father, a masterpiece of its kind. He was energetic, exuberant and egotistical. 'We are all of us worms,' he told Lady Violet Bonham-Carter, 'but I do believe that I am a glow-worm.'

He rose rapidly, reaching one of the goals of his ambition, the Admiralty, in 1911. Four glorious years followed, then the fiasco of the Dardanelles – seemingly the ruin of his career. But he recovered and held high office in the Lloyd George coalition till it crashed in 1922. Out of the House for two years, he went back to his old party and amidst general surprise became Baldwin's Chancellor of the Exchequer from 1924 to 1929, when the Conservatives lost the election. By then he was only fifty-four and had held all the principal offices of state except those of Foreign Secretary and Prime Minister. But his resignation from the shadow cabinet over India in January 1931, scarcely less impetuous than his father's from the real cabinet 44 years earlier, excluded him from the National Coalition formed in August. He was not to hold office again till September 1939.

This unwelcome leisure gave him plenty of time to write. He had already in the 1920s produced his five-volume memoirs of the First World War. He now tackled a theme which he had long considered – a life of the first Duke of Marlborough. It is a notable work in four volumes. The first is the least satisfactory – too polemical about Macaulay who was wrong but not as wrong as Churchill alleged. The ensuing three are masterly. Having finished them he started on his *History of the English-Speaking Peoples,* but laid it aside when war broke out and he returned to the Admiralty for eight months till he became Prime Minister in 1940. This was the apex of his career. If ever words mattered and if ever the man fitted the hour it was then. Churchill's great achievement was to rally the country at a time when victory seemed impossible and defeat highly probable. He certainly infused energy into the prosecution of the war, and, though his strategic decisions and opinions were by no means infallible, he had an unerring ear for what to say and how to say it.

Churchill took enormous trouble about his speeches. He was not a spontaneous orator like Lloyd George. On one occasion as a young man he lost the thread of his discourse and had to sit down in the House without finishing it. After that he learned his words by heart but always had copious notes with which to refresh his memory. Preparation was claimed by one of his acolytes to need an hour for each minute of the delivered speech. This may be an exaggeration, but there can be no doubt about the seriousness with which he regarded the composition of even minor speeches. They took priority over everything else. Disraeli makes a character in one of his novels say: 'With words we govern men.' Churchill certainly made it a guide to his own practice.

He was no less assiduous over his books and articles. He needed money all his life and since writing was his main source he had to be readable. He began as a journalist and continued to write for the press off and on till 1939. There is much to be said for a historian to have experience of reputable journalism. It forces him to be clear, lively and readable. The discipline of the deadline concentrates the mind wonderfully. Churchill wrote against deadlines all his life; and he was always conscious of the need to hold his readership and hence his fees and royalties which over the course of his life amounted to a huge sum. After the debacle of the 1945 election he took up his pen again – the six volumes of his Second World War memoirs. Then came his autumnal second premiership followed by the completion of the *History of the English-Speaking Peoples*. And that was the end.

Churchill was largely self-educated. There were great gaps in his knowledge. He was utterly self-confident, utterly inconsiderate, totally unaware of other people's feelings and strangely unconscious of the adverse reaction which he could and did create among friends as well as foes. But he also inspired great loyalty and affection among people of very diverse outlook and character. One of the qualities which fascinated them and indeed even those who did not normally fall under the enchanter's wand was his ability to enshrine commonplaces in immortal language

He was a great statesman. That is his chief claim to fame. He was also a master of words. That is also a claim to fame, and the two are closely connected. What he said was almost as important as what he did.

Youth & Education

I was happy as a child with my toys in my nursery. I have been happier every year since I became a man. But this interlude of school makes a sombre grey patch upon the chart of my journey.

My Early Life

My nurse [Mrs Everest] was my confidante ... [at her death she was] my dearest and most intimate friend during the whole of the twenty years I had lived. Death came very easily to her. She had lived such an innocent and loving life of service to others, and held such a simple faith, that she had no fears at all and did not seem to mind very much.   *Ibid*

I wrote my name at the top of the page. I wrote down the number of the question '1'. After much reflection, I put a bracket round it thus '(1)'. But thereafter I could not think of anything connected with it that was either relevant or true ... It was from these slender indications of scholarship that Mr Weldon [Headmaster of Harrow] drew the conclusion that I was worthy to pass into Harrow. It was very much to his credit.   *Ibid*

Headmasters have powers at their disposal with which Prime Ministers have never yet been invested.   *Ibid*

I am all for the Public Schools but I do not want to go there again.   *Ibid*

It [school] was an unending spell of worries that did not seem petty, and of toil uncheered by fruition; a time of discomfort, restriction and purposeless monotony.

Ibid

In all the twelve years I was at school no one ever succeeded in making me write a Latin verse or learn any Greek except the alphabet.   *Ibid*

… they told me how Mr. Gladstone read Homer for fun, which I thought served him right.   *Ibid*

They [his school fellows at Harrow] all went on to learn Latin and Greek and splendid things like that. But I was taught English. We were considered such dunces that we could learn only English.   *Ibid*

Hitler … declared that the fight was between those who have been through the Adolf Hitler schools and those who have been at Eton. Hitler has forgotten Harrow …
                    Harrow, 18 Dec. 1940

By being so long in the lowest form [at Harrow] I gained an immense advantage over the cleverer boys … I got into my bones the essential structure of the normal British sentence – which is a noble thing.
                    My Early Life

… I would have liked to have been examined in history, poetry and writing essays. … I should have liked to be asked what I knew. They always tried to ask what I did not know.   *Ibid*

…From time to time I have had to get up disagreeable subjects at short notice, but I consider my triumph, moral and technical, was in learning Mathematics in six months.   *Ibid*

I have never met any of these creatures [cosines and tangents] since. With my third and successful examination they passed away like the phantasmagoria of a fevered dream.   *Ibid*

[Of Bangalore in 1896] It was a curious education. First because I approached it with an empty, hungry mind and with fairly strong jaws; and what I got I bit.   *Ibid*

I could not contemplate toiling [at Oxford in 1899] at Greek irregular verbs after having commanded British regular troops.
                    Ibid

'I presume,' Lord Curzon said to me, 'it will not be long before we hear you declaim in the House of Commons!' Though greatly hampered by inability to compose at the rate necessary for public speaking, I was strongly of the same opinion myself.

Great Contemporaries

Young men have often been ruined through owning horses, or through backing horses, but never through riding them; unless of course they break their necks, which, taken at a gallop, is a very good death to die.

Ibid

I find it poignant to look at youth in all its activity and ardour, and most of all to watch little children playing their merry games, and wonder what would lie before them if God wearied of mankind.

Bardens, *Churchill in Parliament*

Twenty to twenty-five! Those are the years!

My Early Life

My mother made a brilliant impression upon my childhood's life. She shone for me like the Evening Star – I loved her dearly, but at a distance.

Ibid

His father, Lord Randolph Churchill

A swiftly-fading shadow.

Bonham-Carter, *Winston Churchill As I Knew Him*

For years I thought my father with his experience and flair had discerned in me the qualities of military genius. But I was told later that he had only come to the conclusion that I was not clever enough to go to the Bar.

My Early Life

That frail body, driven forward by its nervous energies, had all these last five years been at the utmost strain. Good fortune had sustained it; but disaster, obloquy, and inaction now suddenly descended with crushing force.

Lord Randolph Churchill

All my dreams of comradeship with him, of entering Parliament at his side and in his support, were ended. There remained for me only to pursue his aims and vindicate his memory.

My Early Life

Politics

Some men change their Party for the sake of their principles; others change their principles for the sake of their Party.   1906 General Election

Politics is not a game. It is an earnest business.
                    National Liberal Club, London, 9 Oct. 1909

Politicians rise by toils and struggles. They expect to fall; they hope to rise again.   *Great Contemporaries*

At Sandhurst and in the Army compliments are few and far between ... In politics it was apparently quite different. Here the butter was laid on with a trowel.
                    My Early Life

Most people of common sense know a trade union when they see one. It is like trying to define a rhinoceros: it is difficult enough, but if one is seen, everybody can recognise it.   House of Commons, 25 May 1911

In the present age the State cannot control the Church in spiritual matters; it can only divorce it.
                    House of Commons, 14 June 1928

Whatever one may think of democratic government, it is just as well to have practical experience of its rough and slatternly foundations.
                    Great Contemporaries

I will not pretend that if I had to choose between Communism and Nazism, I would choose Communism. I hope not to be called upon to survive in the world under a Government of either of these dispensations.
                    House of Commons, 14 April 1937

We must build a kind of United States of Europe.
                    Zurich, 19 Sept. 1946

It would be a great reform in politics if wisdom could be made to spread as easily and as rapidly as folly.

Guildhall, London, 10 Sept. 1947

It has been said that Democracy is the worst form of government except all those other forms that have been tried from time to time.

House of Commons, 11 Nov. 1947

Hatred plays the same part in Government as acid in chemistry.

Thoughts and Adventures

The Times is speechless [over Irish Home Rule] and takes three columns to express its speechlessness.

Dundee, 14 May 1908

As to freedom of the press, why should any man be allowed to buy a printing press and disseminate pernicious opinions calculated to embarrass the government?

Brendon, *Winston Churchill*

Free speech carries with it the evil of all foolish, unpleasant, and venomous things that are said, but on the whole we would rather lump them than do away with them.

House of Commons, 15 July 1952

If you substitute violence and clamour for talk, then you are bound to lose the institutions which have always been the glory of the country.

Bardens, *Churchill in Parliament*

I do not like elections, but it is in my many elections that I have learnt to know and honour the people of this island. They are good all through.

Thoughts and Adventures

No part of the education of a politician is more indispensable than the fighting of elections.

Great Contemporaries

[Of the 1922 General Election] In the twinkling of an eye I found myself without an office, without a seat, without a party, and without an appendix.

Thoughts and Adventures

A battle is won and crowds cheer the King. A battle is lost: the Government falls.

Stansky, *Churchill*

[After the General Election in 1945] Why should I accept the Order of the Garter from His Majesty when the people have just given me the order of the boot?

Bardens, *Churchill in Parliament*

The dignity of a Prime Minister, like a lady's virtue, was not susceptible of partial diminution.

House of Commons, 24 July 1905

Don't get torpedoed, for if I am left alone your colleagues will eat me.

Letter to Lloyd George, 1916

If he [the Prime Minister] trips he must be sustained. If he makes mistakes they must be covered. If he sleeps he must not be wantonly disturbed. If he is no good he must be pole-axed.

The Second World War, vol. 2

When I was called upon to be Prime Minister, now nearly two years ago, there were not many applicants for the job. Since then perhaps the market has improved.

House of Commons, 27 Jan. 1942

Socialism

Socialism attacks capital; Liberalism attacks monopoly. Socialism seeks to pull down wealth; Liberalism seeks to raise up poverty. Dundee, 14 May 1908

If you strike at savings you at once propagate the idea of 'Let us eat, drink and be merry, for tomorrow we die'. That is at once the inspiration and the mortal disease by which the Socialist philosophy is affected.
House of Commons, 19 May 1927

Socialism is inseparably interwoven with totalitarianism and the abject worship of the State. Look how even to-day they [the Socialists] hunger for controls of every kind as if these were delectable foods instead of wartime inflictions. ... This State is to be the arch-employer, the arch-planner, the arch-administrator and ruler, and the arch-caucus-boss.
Broadcast, 4 June 1945

No Socialist system can be established without a political police. ... They would have to fall back on some form of Gestapo – no doubt very humanely directed in the first instance. *Ibid*

The inherent vice of Capitalism is the unequal sharing of blessings; the inherent virtue of Socialism is the equal sharing of miseries.
House of Commons, 22 Oct. 1945

When this new Parliament first met all the Socialist Members stood up and sang the 'Red Flag' in their triumph. Peering ahead through the mists and mysteries of the future ... I see the division at the next election will be between those who wholeheartedly sing the 'Red Flag' and those who rejoice to sing 'Land of Hope and Glory'.
Blackpool, 5 Oct. 1946

The German U-boats in their worst endeavour never made bread rationing necessary in war. It took a Socialist Government and Socialist planners to fasten it on us in time of peace when the seas are open and the harvests good.

Ibid

And now the British housewife, as she stands in the queues to buy her bread ration, will fumble in her pocket in vain for a silver sixpence. Under the Socialist Government nickel will have to be good enough for her. In future we shall still be able to say: 'Every cloud has a nickel lining.'

Blackpool, 5 Oct. 1946

They want to reduce us to one vast Wormwood Scrubbery.

House of Commons, 12 March 1947

The Socialist dream is no longer Utopia but Queuetopia. And if they have the power this part of their dream will certainly come true.

Woodford, 28 Jan. 1950

Parliament

[Of his maiden speech] I came with a quiverful of arrows of different patterns and sizes, some of which I hoped would hit the target.

My Early Life

If I had to choose between the interests of the dignity of the House of Commons and its freedom I would pronounce for its freedom. It would not enjoy real dignity unless its debates were free.

House of Commons, 15 March 1905

The House of Commons is a jealous mistress: you must give her the cream of your thought.

Ibid

I never complain of hard words across the floor of the House, but I claim to be allowed to match them with arguments equal to the attack which has been made.

House of Commons, 4 April 1911

Parliament can compel people to obey or to submit, but it cannot compel them to agree.

House of Commons, 27 Sept. 1926

Five or ten years' experience as a Member of this House is as fine an all-round education in public affairs as any man can obtain.

House of Commons, 27 Feb. 1941

There is no situation to which it [the House of Commons] cannot address itself with vigour and ingenuity. It is the citadel of British liberty. It is the foundation of our laws.

House of Commons, 23 Oct. 1942

[The House of Commons] is always indulgent to those who are proud to be its servants.

My Early Life

The essence and foundation of House of Commons debating is formal conversation. The set speech, the harangues addressed to constituents, or to the wider public out of doors, has never succeeded much in our small, wisely built chamber.   *Great Contemporaries*

[The House of Commons'] structure has stood the strain of the most violent contentions. Its long tradition, its collective personality, its flexible procedure, its social life, its unwritten inviolable conventions have made an organism more effective for the purpose of assimilation than any of which there is record.

Thoughts and Adventures

It must be remembered that the function of Parliament is not only to pass good laws, but to stop bad laws.

House of Commons, 4 April 1944

[On rebuilding the House] We shape our dwellings, and afterwards our dwellings shape us.

House of Commons, 28 Oct. 1944

[To an MP after defeat on the Education Bill 1944] I am not going to tumble round my cage like a wounded canary. You knocked me off my perch. You have now to put me back on my perch. Otherwise I won't sing.

Nicolson, *Diaries and Letters*

I have lived in the House of Commons, having served there for fifty-two of the fifty-four years of this tumultuous and convulsive century. ... I have never ceased to love the Mother of Parliaments, the model to the legislative assemblies of so many lands.

London, 30 Nov. 1954

The House of Lords

A lingering relic of a feudal order   *The People's Rights*

… this Second Chamber as it is – one-sided, hereditary, unpurged, unrepresentative, irresponsible, absentee.
House of Commons, 29 June 1907

… there are 400 or 500 backwoodsmen Peers, all meditating on their estates on the great questions of Government, all studying *Ruff's Guide* and other blue books, all revolving the problems of Empire and Epsom, everyone of them a heaven-born, God-granted legislator.
The People's Rights

These unfortunate individuals [the Lords] who ought to lead quiet, delicate, sheltered lives, far from the madding crowd's ignoble strife, have been dragged into the football scrimmage, and they have got rather roughly mauled in the process….
Leicester, 4 Sept. 1909

It is a poor sport [attacking the Lords] – almost like teasing goldfish … there is no sport whatever in catching them. It would be barbarous to leave them gasping on the bank of public ridicule upon which they have landed themselves. Let us put them back gently, tenderly into their fountains – and if a few bright scales have been rubbed off in what the Prime Minister calls the variegated handling they have received, they will soon get over it.
Ibid

Contemporaries

To do justice to a great man, discriminating criticism is necessary. Gush, however quenching, is always insipid.

Marchant, *Winston Spencer Churchill*

H.H. Asquith

…Probably one of the greatest Prime Ministers we ever had.

Great Contemporaries

The phrase 'Wait and see' which he had used in peace, not indeed in a dilatory but in a minatory sense, reflected with injustice, but with just enough truth to be dangerous, upon his name and policy.

Ibid

The difference between him and Arthur [Balfour] is that Arthur is wicked and moral, Asquith is good and immoral.

Raymond, *Mr Balfour*

Lady Astor

She combines a kindly heart with a sharp and wagging tongue … She denounces the vice of gambling in unmeasured terms and is closely associated with an almost unrivalled racing stable. She accepts Communist hospitality and flattery and remains the Conservative member for Plymouth … She does all the opposite things so well and so naturally that the public, tired of criticising, can only gape.

Great Contemporaries

Clement Attlee

If you feed a grub on royal jelly you may turn it into a queen bee.

Brendon, *Winston Churchill*

Mr Attlee combines a limited outlook with strong qualities of resistance.

Royal Albert Hall, London, 27 April 1951

A sheep in sheep's clothing.   Attrib.

Stanley Baldwin

In those days Mr Baldwin was wiser than he is now; he used frequently to take my advice.

House of Commons, 22 May 1935

He occasionally stumbled over the truth, but hastily picked himself up and hurried on as if nothing had happened.

Attrib.

When I first went into Parliament, now nearly forty years ago.... the most insulting charge which could be made against a Minister ... short of actual malfeasance, was that he had endangered the safety of the country ... for electioneering consideration. Yet such are the surprising qualities of Mr Baldwin that what all had been taught to shun has now been elevated into a canon of political virtue.

Letter, 11 Dec. 1936

A.J. Balfour

A taste most truly refined, a judgement comprehensively balanced, an insight penetrating, a passion cold, long, slow, unyielding – all these were his.

Great Contemporaries

His aversion from the Roman Catholic faith was dour and inveterate. Otherwise he seemed to have the personal qualifications of a great Pope ... He was quite fearless ... Poverty never entered his thoughts. Disgrace was impossible because of his character and behaviour.

Ibid

Max Beaverbrook

Some people take drugs, I take Max.

Brendon, *Winston Churchill*

Lord Charles Beresford

He can best be described as one of those orators who, before they get up, do not know what they are going to say; when they are speaking, do not know what they are saying; and, when they have sat down, do not know what they have said.

Speech after his appointment to the Admiralty, 1911

Aneurin Bevan

He will be as great a curse to this country in peace, as he was a squalid nuisance in war.

House of Commons, 1945

There is ... a poetic justice in the fact that the most mischievous mouth in wartime has become in peace the most remarkable administrative failure.

Blackpool, 5 Oct. 1946

Rupert Brooke

[On his death in 1915] A voice had become audible, a note had been struck, more true, more thrilling ... than any other ... The voice has been swiftly stilled.

Bonham-Carter, *Winston Churchill As I Knew Him*

Joseph Chamberlain

One mark of a great man is the power of making lasting impressions upon people he meets ... He lighted beacon fires which are still burning; he sounded trumpet calls whose echoes still call stubborn soldiers to the field.

Great Contemporaries

At the time when I looked out of my regimental cradle and was thrilled by politics he was incomparably the most lively, sparkling, insurgent, compulsive figure in British affairs.

Ibid

Radicalism was his warhorse, municipal politics the stirrup by which he mounted to the saddle.

Ibid

Stafford Cripps

Neither of his colleagues can compare with him in that acuteness and energy of mind with which he devotes himself to so many topics injurious to the strength and welfare of the state.

House of Commons, 1946

There but for the grace of God goes God.

Brendon, *Winston Churchill*

R.H.S. Crossman

The Hon. Member is never lucky in the coincidence of his facts with the truth.

House of Commons, 14 July 1954

Lord Curzon

His facility carried him with a bound into prolixity; his ceremonious diction wore the aspect of pomposity; his wide knowledge was accused of superficiality; his natural pre-eminence was accompanied by airs of superiority.

Great Contemporaries

He aroused both admiration and envy, but neither much love nor much hatred. *Ibid*

Hugh Dalton

The practitioner who never cured anyone.

London, 14 Feb. 1948

Charles de Gaulle

In the last four years I have had many differences with General de Gaulle, but I have never forgotten, and can never forget, that he stood forth as the first eminent Frenchman to face the common foe in what seemed to be the hour of ruin of his country, and possibly of ours.

House of Commons, 2 Aug. 1944

John Foster Dulles

Dull, duller, Dulles.

Brendon, *Winston Churchill*

Edward VIII

I should have been ashamed if, in my independent and unofficial position, I had not cast about for every lawful means, even the most folorn, to keep him on the throne of his fathers.

Bardens, *Churchill in Parliament*

Elizabeth II

I, whose youth was passed in the august, unchallenged and tranquil glories of the Victorian era, may well feel a thrill in invoking GOD SAVE THE QUEEN! ... She comes to this throne at a time when tormented mankind stands uncertainly poised between catastrophe and a golden age.

Broad, *Winston Churchill*

Marshal Foch

He began his career a little cub, brushed aside by the triumphant march of the German armies to Paris and victory; he lived to see all the might of valiant Germany prostrate and suppliant at his pencil tip.

Great Contemporaries

Mahatma Gandhi

It is alarming and also nauseating to see Mr Gandhi, a seditious Middle Temple lawyer, now posing as a fakir ..., striding half naked up the steps of the Viceregal palace ... to parley on equal terms with the representative of the King-Emperor.

Epping, 25 Feb. 1931

George VI

We thought of him so faithful in his study and discharge
of State affairs, so strong in his devotion to the enduring
honour of our country, so self-restained in his
judgement of men and affairs, so uplifted above the
clash of party politics, yet so attentive to them; so wise
and shrewd in judging what matters and what does not.

Broadcast, 7 Feb. 1952

General Gordon

A man careless alike of the frowns of men or the smiles
of women, of life or comfort, wealth or fame.

The River War

Rudolf Hess

He is the maggot in the Nazi apple.

Eden, *Portrait of Churchill*

Adolf Hitler

He it was who exorcised the spirit of despair from the
German mind by substituting the not less baleful but far
less morbid spirit of revenge.

Great Contemporaries

A boa constrictor, who had already covered his prey
with his foul saliva and then had it suddenly wrested
from his coils, would be in an amicable mood compared
with Hitler.   House of Commons, 9 April 1941

At four o'clock this morning Hitler attacked and
invaded Russia. All his usual formalities of perfidy were
observed with scrupulous technique.

Broadcast, 22 June 1941

A monster of wickedness, insatiable in his lust for blood
and plunder.   Broadcast, 26 June 1941

This bloodthirsty guttersnipe.   *Ibid*

I always hate to compare Napoleon with Hitler, as it seems an insult to the great Emperor and warrior to compare him in any way with a squalid caucus boss and butcher.

House of Commons, Sept. 1944

Lord Jellicoe

He was the only man on either side who could lose the war in an afternoon.

The World Crisis

Lawrence of Arabia

From amid the flowing draperies his noble features, his perfectly chiselled lips and flashing eyes loaded with fire and comprehension shone forth. He looked what he was, one of Nature's greatest princes.

Great Contemporaries

V.I. Lenin

Lenin was sent to Russia by the Germans in the same way that you might send a phial containing a culture of typhoid or cholera to be poured into the water supply of a great city, and it worked with amazing accuracy.

House of Commons, 5 Nov. 1919

He alone could have led Russia into the enchanted quagmire: he alone could have found the way back to the causeway. He saw; he turned; he perished ... The Russian people were left floundering in the bog. Their worst misfortune was his birth, their next worst – his death.

The World Crisis

David Lloyd George

At his best he could almost talk a bird out of a tree.

Thoughts and Adventures

How could Count Metternich know what Mr Lloyd George was going to do? Until a few hours before, his colleagues did not know. Working with him in close association, I did not know. No one knew. Until his mind was definitely made up, he did not know himself.

The World Crisis

He was foolish to throw me over, for together we were a power.

Martin Gilbert, *Winston Churchill*, Companion to vol. 4

The Happy Warrior of Squandermania.

House of Commons, 15 April 1929

Lord Kitchener

I cannot forget that when I left the Admiralty in May 1915 the first and, with one exception, only one of my colleagues who paid me a visit of ceremony was the overburdened Titan whose disapprobation had been one of the disconcerting experiences of my youth.

The World Crisis

David Low

Low is a master of black and white; he is the Charlie Chaplin of caricature, and tragedy and comedy are the same to him.

Thoughts and Adventures

You cannot bridle the wild ass of the desert, still less prohibit its natural hee-haw.

Ibid

Ramsay MacDonald

I remember when I was a child, being taken to the celebrated Barnum's Circus, which contained an exhibition of freaks and monstrosities, but the exhibit on the programme which I most desired to see was the one described as 'The Boneless Wonder'. My parents judged that the spectacle would be too revolting and demoralising for my youthful eyes, and I have waited fifty years to see the Boneless Wonder sitting on the Treasury Bench.

House of Commons, 28 Jan. 1931

He has, more than any other man, the gift of compressing the largest amount of words into the smallest amount of thought.

House of Commons, 23 March 1933

V.M. Molotov

I have never seen a human being who more perfectly represented the modern conception of a robot.

The Second World War, vol. 1

Viscount Montgomery

This vehement and formidable General – a Cromwellian figure – austere, severe, accomplished, tireless – his life given to the study of war, who has attracted to himself in an extraordinary degree the confidence and devotion of the Army.

House of Commons, Feb. 1943

Lord Morley

To me when I first saw it, John Morley's 'modest rushlight' had become a very bright ray. I admired it without seeking to borrow its flame. I approached near enough to read by its light, and to feel its agreeable, genial, companionable warmth.   *Great Contemporaries*

Six years of constant, friendly and to me stimulating propinquity!   *Ibid*

Sir Oswald Mosley

A gilded butterfly.

Brendon, *Winston Churchill*

Benito Mussolini

This whipped jackal, Mussolini, is frisking up by the side of the German tiger with yelps not only of appetite – that could be understood – but even of triumph.

House of Commons, April 1941

... the crafty, coldblooded, black-hearted Italian.

Bardens, *Churchill in Parliament*

Lord Rosebery

It might be said that Lord Rosebery outlived his future by ten years and his past by more than twenty.

Great Contemporaries

President Roosevelt

I shall not hesitate to affirm, and indeed to repeat, that he was the greatest American friend that Britain ever found, and the foremost champion of freedom and justice who has ever stretched strong hands across the oceans to rescue Europe and Asia from tyranny and destruction.

Savoy Hotel, London, 12 April 1948

That great man whom destiny has marked for this climax of human fortune.

Canadian Parliament at Ottawa, 30 Dec. 1941

George Bernard Shaw

He was one of my earliest antipathies … I possess a
lively image of this bright, nimble, fierce and
comprehending being, Jack Frost dancing bespangled in
the sunshine. He is at once an acquisitive Capitalist and
a sincere Communist. He makes his characters talk
blithely about killing men for the sake of an idea; but
would take great trouble not to hurt a fly.

Great Contemporaries

Certainly we are all the better for having had the Jester
in our midst. *Ibid*

Saint, sage and clown; venerable, profound and
irrepressible … *Ibid*

Sir Hartley Shawcross

Sir Shortly Floorcross. Brendon, *Winston Churchill*

F.E. Smith

F.E. had a complete armoury. The bludgeon for the
platform, the rapier for a personal dispute, the
entangling net and the unexpected trident for the Courts
of Law and a jug of clear spring water for an anxious
perplexed conclave. *Great Contemporaries*

He had all the canine virtues in a remarkable degree –
courage, fidelity, vigilance, love of the chase. *Ibid*

Philip Snowden

He was really a tender-hearted man, who would not
have hurt a gnat unless his party and the Treasury told
him to do so, and then only with compunction. *Ibid*

A perverse destiny has seemed to brood over the right
hon. gentleman's career; all his life has been one long
struggle to overcome the natural amiability of his
character. House of Commons, 25 May 1925

Joseph Stalin

A hard-boiled egg of a man ... At once a callous, a crafty and an ill-formed man.

Brendon, *Winston Churchill*

Leon Trotsky

He sits disconsolate – a skin of malice stranded for a time on the shores of the Black Sea and now washed up in the Gulf of Mexico. He possessed in his nature all the qualities requisite for the art of civic destruction – the organising command of a Carnot, the cold detached intelligence of a Machiavelli, the mob oratory of a Cleon, the ferocity of a Jack the Ripper, the toughness of Titus Oates.

Great Contemporaries

In the deepest depth he sought with desperate energy for a deeper. But – poor wretch – he had reached rock bottom. Nothing lower than the Communist criminal class could be found.

Ibid

I must confess that I never liked Trotsky.

House of Commons, Aug. 1944

President Wilson

The inscrutable and undecided judge upon whose lips the lives of millions hung.

The World Crisis

War

The story of the human race is War. Except for brief and precarious interludes, there has never been peace in the world.

The World Crisis

In war, which is an intense form of life, chance casts aside all veils and disguises and presents herself nakedly from moment to moment as the direct arbiter over all persons and events.

Thoughts and Adventures

War, which used to be cruel and magnificent, has now become cruel and squalid. In fact it has been completely spoilt. It is all the fault of Democracy and Science.

My Early Life

War, disguise it as you may, is but a dirty, shoddy business, which only a fool would play at.

Manchester, *The Caged Lion*

In war, the clouds never blow over; they gather unceasingly and fall in thunderbolts.

The World Crisis

A single glass of champagne imparts a feeling of exhilaration. The nerves are braced; the imagination is agreeably stirred; the wits become more nimble. A bottle produces a contrary effect. Excess causes a comotosed insensibility. So it is with war; and the quality of both is best discovered by sipping.

The Malakand Field Force

Let us learn our lessons. Never, never, never believe any war will be smooth and easy ... Always remember, however sure you are that you can easily win, that there would not be a war if the other man did not think he also had a chance.

My Early Life

This truth is incontrovertible [the superiority of the aeroplane over the airship]. Panic may resent it; ignorance may deride it; malice may distort it; but there it is.

House of Commons, 17 May 1915

Never has the human race displayed the fortitude which was the ordinary habit of the men of the Great War.

Thoughts and Adventures

In wartime ... truth is so precious that she should always be attended by a bodyguard of lies.

The Second World War, vol. 5

Battles are won by slaughter and manoeuvre. The greater the general, the more he contributes in manoeuvre, the less he demands in slaughter.

The World Crisis

When the advance of destructive weapons enables us to kill everybody else nobody will want to kill anybody at all.

Brendon, *Winston Churchill*

In an aerial war the greatest form of defence will undoubtedly be offence.

House of Commons, 21 Mar. 1922

The flying peril is not a peril from which one can fly. We cannot possibly retreat. We cannot move London.

House of Commons, 28 Nov. 1934

Dictators ride to and fro upon tigers which they dare not dismount. And the tigers are getting hungry.

While England Slept

[After Munich] England has been offered a choice between war and shame. She has chosen shame but she will get war.

House of Commons, Sept. 1938

[On the invasion of Czechoslovakia] All is over. Silent, mournful, abandoned, broken, Czechoslovakia recedes into the darkness ... We have sustained a defeat without a war.

House of Commons, 5 Oct. 1938

[On the capture of Prague] This damnable outrage opened the eyes of the blind, made the deaf hear, and even in some cases the dumb spoke.

Corn Exchange, Cambridge, 19 May 1939

Poland has been again overrun by two of the great powers which held her in bondage for 150 years, but were unable to quench the spirit of the Polish nation. The heroic defence of Warsaw shows that the soul of Poland is indestructible, and that she will rise again like a rock, which may for a spell be submerged by a tidal wave, but which remains a rock.   London, 1 Oct. 1939

[I was] conscious of a profound source of relief. I felt as if I was walking with destiny, and that all my past life had been but a preparation for this hour and this trial.

10 May 1940, as Prime Minister

I have nothing to offer but blood, toil, tears and sweat.

House of Commons, 13 May 1940

Victory, victory at all costs, victory in spite of all terror, victory however long and hard the road might be; for without victory there is no survival.   *Ibid*

Our task is not only to win the battle – but to win the war.   Broadcast, 19 May 1940

We shall go on to the end, we shall fight in France, we shall fight on the seas and oceans, we shall fight with growing confidence and growing strength in the air, we shall defend our island, whatever the cost may be, we shall fight on the beaches, we shall fight on the landing grounds, we shall fight in the fields and in the streets, we shall fight in the hills; we shall never surrender.

House of Commons, 4 June 1940

If we open a quarrel between the past and present, we shall find that we have lost the future.

House of Commons, 18 June 1940

Let us therefore brace ourselves to our duties, and so bear ourselves that, if the British Empire and its Commonwealth last for a thousand years, men will still say: 'This was their finest hour.'

Ibid

[On being bombed] Learn to get used to it. Eels get used to skinning. Notes for a speech, 20 June 1940

[On meat rationing] Almost all the food faddists I have ever known, nut eaters and the like, have died very young after a long period of senile decay. The British soldier is far more likely to be right than the scientists. All he cares about is beef ...

Colville, *The Fringes of Power*

[After Dunkirk] There was a white glow, overpowering, sublime, which ran through our island from end to end.

Stansky, *Churchill*

Never in the field of human conflict was so much owed by so many to so few.

House of Commons, 20 Aug. 1940

Death and sorrow will be the companions of our journey; hardship our garment; constancy and valour our only shield. We must be united, we must be undaunted, we must be inflexible.

House of Commons, 8 Oct. 1940

We are waiting for the long-promised invasion. So are the fishes.

Broadcast to the French people, 21 Oct. 1940

If this long island story of ours is to end at last let it end only when each one of us lies choking in his own blood upon the ground.

Brendon, *Winston Churchill*

What he [Hitler] has done is to kindle a fire in British hearts, here and all over the world, which will glow long after all traces of the conflagrations in London have been destroyed.

Eden, *Portrait of Churchill*

[Addressing President Roosevelt] We shall not fail or falter; we shall not weaken or tire. Neither the sudden shock of battle, nor the long-drawn trials of vigilance and exertion will wear us down. Give us the tools, and we will finish the job.

Broadcast, 9 Feb. 1941

[Of the German attack on Russia in June 1941] We are in the presence of a crime without a name.

Broad, *Winston Churchill*

If we win nobody will care. If we lose, there will be nobody to care.

House of Commons, 25 June 1941

Do not let us speak of darker days; let us rather speak of sterner days. These are not dark days: these are great days – the greatest days our country has ever lived; and we must all thank God that we have been allowed, each of us according to our stations, to play a part in making these days memorable in the history of our race.

Harrow School, 29 Oct. 1941

[On the declaration of war against Japan, 8 Dec. 1941] When you have to kill a man, it costs nothing to be polite.

The Second World War, vol. 3

When I warned them [the French Government] that Britain would fight on alone, whatever they did, their Generals told their Prime Minister and his divided Cabinet: 'In three weeks England will have her neck wrung like a chicken.' Some chicken! Some neck!

Canadian Parliament, 30 Dec. 1941

Our defeats are but stepping stones to victory, and his [Hitler's] victories are but stepping stones to ruin.

Edinburgh, 12 Oct. 1942

[Of the Battle of Egypt] This is not the end. It is not even the beginning of the end. But it is, perhaps, the end of the beginning.

Mansion House, 10 Nov. 1942

The soft under-belly of the Axis.

House of Commons, 11 Nov. 1942

The proud German Army by its sudden collapse, sudden crumbling and breaking up, has once again proved the truth of the saying 'The Hun is always either at your throat or at your feet'.

US Congress, 19 May 1943

It is a poor heart that never rejoices; but our thanksgiving, however fervent, must be brief.   *Ibid*

[On the Chiefs of Staff system, 16 Nov. 1943] You may take the most gallant sailor, the most intrepid airman, or the most audacious soldier, put them at a table together – what do you get? *The sum of their fears*.

Macmillan, *The Blast of War*

[On seeing a film of Allied bombing] Are we beasts? Are we taking this a bit too far?

Brendon, *Winston Churchill*

War is a hard school, but the British, once compelled to get there, are attentive pupils.

House of Commons, 2 Aug. 1944

The bomb bought peace, but man alone can keep that peace.   House of Commons, 16 Aug. 1945

The air is an extremely dangerous, jealous and exacting mistress. Once under the spell most lovers are faithful to the end, which is not always old age.

Thoughts and Adventures

The RAF is the cavalry of modern war.

Stansky, *Churchill*

On the night of the tenth of May [1940], at the outset of this mighty battle, I acquired the chief power in the State, which henceforth I wielded in ever-growing measure for five years and three months of world war, at the end of which time, all our enemies having surrendered unconditionally or being about to do so, I was immediately dismissed by the British electorate from all further conduct of their affairs.

The Second World War, vol. 1

Twice the United States has had to send several million of its young men across the Atlantic to find the war; but now war can find any nation, wherever it may dwell, between dusk and dawn.   Fulton, Missouri, 5 March 1946.

Nothing is more costly, nothing is more sterile, than vengeance.   House of Commons, 5 June 1946

I was all for war. Now I am all for peace.

Marchant, *Winston Spencer Churchill*

In making an army, three elements are necessary – men, weapons and money. There must also be time.

House of Commons, 1 Dec. 1948

It was the nation and the race dwelling all round the globe that had the lion's heart. I had the luck to be called upon to give the roar.   Palace of Westminster, 30 Nov. 1954

The day may dawn when fair play, love for one's fellow men, respect for justice and freedom will enable tormented generations to march forth serene and triumphant from the hideous epoch in which we have to dwell. Meanwhile never flinch, never weary, never despair.   House of Commons, 1 Mar. 1955

[On the Suez crisis] I am not sure I should have dared to start, but I am sure I should not have dared to stop.

Thomas, *The Suez Affair*

History

History with its flickering lamp stumbles along the trail of the past, trying to reconstruct its scenes, to revive its echoes, and kindle with pale gleams the passion of former days.

House of Commons, 12 May 1940

In the long story of a nation we often see that capable rulers by their very virtues sow the seeds of future evil and weak or degenerate princes open the path of progress.

History of the English-Speaking Peoples, vol. 1

No one can understand history without continually relating the long periods which are constantly mentioned to the experience of our brief lives. Five years is a lot. Twenty years is the horizon ... Fifty years is antiquity.

Ibid

The great struggles in history have been won by superior will-power wresting victory in the teeth of odds or upon the narrowest of margins.

House of Commons, 25 June 1941

It has been said that the dominant lesson of history is that mankind is unteachable.

The General Assembly of Virginia, Richmond, 8 March 1946

I consider that it will be found much better by all parties [of the House of Commons] to leave the past to history, especially as I propose to write that history myself.

House of Commons, 1948

Give me the facts, Ashley [his research assistant], and I will twist them the way I want to suit my argument.

M. Ashley, *Churchill as Historian*

Britain & The Empire

The maxim of the British people is 'Business as usual.'

Guildhall, London, 9 Nov. 1914

Nothing can save England if she will not save herself. If we lose faith in ourselves, in our capacity to guide and govern, if we lose our will to live, then, indeed our story is told.

Bardens, *Churchill in Parliament*

Frightfulness is not a remedy known to the British pharmacopoeia.

House of Commons, 8 July 1920

It makes me sick when I hear the Secretary of State saying of India '*she* will do this and *she* will do that'. India is an abstraction ... India is no more a political personality than Europe. India is a geographical term. It is no more a united nation than the Equator.

Albert Hall, 18 March 1931

Gandhi stands for the expulsion of Britain from India. Gandhi stands for the permanent exclusion of British trade from India. Gandhi stands for the substitution of Brahmin domination for British rule in India. You will never be able to come to terms with Gandhi.   *Ibid*

All sorts of greedy appetites have been excited, and many itching fingers are stretching and scratching at the vast pillage of a derelict Empire.   *Ibid*

I have watched this famous island descending incontinently, recklessly, the stairway which leads to a dark gulf. It is a fine broad stairway at the beginning, but, after a bit, the carpet ends. A little further on there are only flagstones, and, a little further on still, these break beneath your feet.

While England Slept

We should lay aside every hindrance; and endeavour, by uniting the whole force and spirit of our people, to raise again a great British nation standing up before all the world. For such a nation, rising in its ancient vigour, can even at this hour save civilisation.

House of Commons, 24 March 1938

The British Empire and the United States will have to be somewhat mixed up together in some of their affairs for mutual and general advantage. For my own part, looking out for the future, I do not view the process with any misgivings. I could not stop it if I wished; no one can stop it. Like the Mississippi, it just keeps rolling along. Let it roll. Let it roll in full flood, inexorable, irresistible, benignant, to broader lands and better days.

House of Commons, 20 Aug. 1940

The British nation is unique in this respect. They are the only people who like to be told how bad things are, who like to be told the worst, and like to be told that they are very likely to get much worse in the future ...

House of Commons, 10 June 1941

I have not become the King's First Minister in order to preside over the liquidation of the British Empire.

Mansion House, 10 Nov. 1942

[On news of the collapse of Japan] Once again the British Commonwealth and Empire emerges safe, undiminished, and united from a mortal struggle. Monstrous tyrannies which menaced our life have been beaten to the ground in ruin, and a brighter radiance illumines the Imperial Crown than any which our annals record.

House of Commons, 15 Aug. 1945

In England the political opinion of men and parties grows like a tree shading its trunk with its branches, shaped or twisted by the winds, rooted according to its strains, stunted by drought or maimed by storms.

Thoughts and Adventures

Upon Britain fell the proud but awful responsibility of keeping the Flag of Freedom flying in the Old World till the forces of the New World arrived.

Brussels, 16 Nov. 1945

It is with deep grief that I watch the clattering down of the British Empire ... Many have defended Britain against her foes. None can defend her against herself.

House of Commons, 6 March 1947

It is always, I think, true to say that one of the main foundations of the British sense of humour is understatement.

House of Commons, 27 July 1950

No country in the world is less fitted for a conflict with terrorists than Great Britain, not because of weakness and cowardice, but because of our restraint and our virtues.

Bardens, *Churchill in Parliament*

England's hour of weakness is Europe's hour of danger.

Manchester, *The Caged Lion*

The British people are good all through. You can test them as you would put a bucket into the sea and always find it salt.

The Second World War, vol. 1

America

I have learnt to admire the courtesy of these audiences [in America]; their sense of fair play; their sovereign sense of humour, never minding the joke that is turned against themselves; their earnest, voracious desire to come to the root of the matter, and to be well and truly informed on Old World affairs.

London, 16 June 1941

Should the United States become involved in war with Japan, the British declaration will follow within the hour.

Mansion House, 20 Nov. 1941

[After Pearl Harbor, December 1941] So we had won after all.

Brendon, *Winston Churchill*

Oh! that is the way we talked to her [the USA in 1941] while we were wooing her; now that she is in the harem we talk to her quite differently.

Ibid

In my country, as in yours, public men are proud to be servants of the state and would be ashamed to be its masters.

US Congress, 26 Dec. 1941

I cannot help reflecting that if my father had been an American and my mother British, instead of the other way round, I might have got here on my own.

US Congress, 1941

The experience of a long life and the promptings of my blood have wrought in me the conviction that there is nothing more important for the future of the world than the fraternal association of our two peoples in righteous work both in war and peace.

Broadcast, Washington DC, 19 May 1943

[On Anglo-American co-operation] If we are together nothing is impossible, and if we are divided all will fail.

Harvard, Aug. 1943

The United States is a land of free speech. Nowhere is speech freer – not even here where we sedulously cultivate it even in its most repulsive form.

House of Commons, 28 Sept. 1944

There have been many occasions when a powerful state has wished to raise great armies, and with money and time and discipline and loyalty that can be accomplished. Nevertheless the rate at which the small American Army of only a few hundred thousand men, not long before the war, created the mighty force of millions of soldiers, is a wonder in military history.

Pentagon, 9 March 1946

We must also never allow ... the growing sense of unity and brotherhood between the United Kingdom and the United States and throughout the English-speaking world to be injured or retarded.

House of Commons, 1 March 1955

Russia

Bolshevism is a great evil, but it has arisen out of great social evils.

House of Commons, 29 May 1919

Here we have a State whose subjects are so happy that they have to be forbidden to quit its bounds under the direst penalties ...   House of Commons, 29 July 1919

In Russia a man is called a reactionary if he objects to having his property stolen and his wife and children murdered.   House of Commons, 5 Nov. 1919

I cannot forecast to you the action of Russia. It is a riddle wrapped in a mystery inside an enigma.

Broadcast, 1 Oct. 1939

[On dicovering that his Russian villa was bugged] The Russians, I have been told, are not human beings at all. They are lower on the scale of nature than the orang-outang. Now then, let them take that down and translate it into Russian.

Brendon, *Winston Churchill*

[On the visit of George Bernard Shaw and Lady Astor to Russia] The Russians have always been fond of circuses and travelling shows ... And here was the World's most famous intellectual Clown and Pantaloon in one, and the charming Columbine of the capitalist pantomime.

Great Contemporaries

Everybody has always underestimated the Russians. They keep their own secrets alike from foe and friends.

House of Commons, 23 April 1942

I feel like telling the Russians that personally I fight tyranny whatever uniform it wears or slogans it utters.

Stansky, *Churchill*

[Of his visit to Stalin in 1942] Like carrying a large lump of ice to the North Pole.

Brendon, *Winston Churchill*

What can we do to help Russia? There is nothing that we would not do. If the sacrifice of thousands of British lives would turn the scale, our fellow countrymen would not flinch.

House of Commons, 26 April 1942

There is a winter, you know, in Russia ... Hitler forgot about this Russian winter. He must have been very loosely educated. We all heard about it at school; but he forgot it. I have never made such a bad mistake as that.

Broadcast, 10 May 1942

We are sea animals, and the United States are to a large extent ocean animals. The Russians are land animals. Happily, we are all three air animals.

House of Commons, 8 Sept. 1942

[Pointing East in a Parisian street in the late 1940s] Russia! Russia! That's where the weather is coming from.

Marchant, *Winston Spencer Churchill*

From Strettin in the Baltic to Trieste in the Adriatic an iron curtain is descending across the Continent ...

Fulton, Missouri, 5 March 1946

Let there be sunshine on both sides of the iron curtain; and if ever the sunshine should be equal on both sides, the curtain will be no more.

Blenheim, 4 Aug. 1947

[In March 1950] I think it is probable that Soviet governments fear the friendship of the West even more than they do our hostility.

Broad, *Winston Churchill*

Foreigners

Everybody has the right to pronounce foreign names as he chooses.

Observer, 5 Aug. 1951

The Arab was an African reproduction of the Englishman; the Englishman a superior and civilised development of the Arab.

The River War

France, though armed to the teeth, is pacifist to the core.

House of Commons, 23 Nov. 1932

For good or for ill the French people have been effective masters in their own house, and have built as they chose upon the ruins of the old regime. They have done what they like. Their difficulty is to like what they have done.

Letter, 18 Sept. 1936

The Almighty in his infinite wisdom did not see fit to create Frenchmen in the image of Englishmen.

House of Commons, 10 Dec. 1942

We shall continue to operate on the Italian donkey at both ends – with a carrot and with a stick.

US Press Conference, May 1943

[Discussing Eisenhower's designs against Sardinia] I refuse to be fobbed off with a Sardine.

Brendon, *Winston Churchill*

The Japanese, whose game is what I may call to make hell while the sun shines ...

House of Commons, 27 Jan. 1942

There are few virtues that the Poles do not possess – and there are few mistakes they have ever avoided.

House of Commons, 16 Aug. 1945.

Books & Painting

I would make boys all learn English; and then I would let the clever ones learn Latin as an honour and Greek as a treat. But the only thing I would whip them for is not knowing English. I would whip them hard for that.

My Early Life

The man who cannot say what he has to say in good English cannot have very much to say that is worth listening to.

Manchester, *The Caged Lion*

Men will forgive a man anything except bad prose.

Manchester, 1906

Books in all their variety are often the means by which civilisation may be carried triumphantly forward.

Ministry of Information Film, 1941

It is a great pity to read a book too soon in life ... Young people should be careful in their reading, as old people in eating their food. They should not eat too much. They should chew it well.

Thoughts and Adventures

Short words are best and the old words when short are the best of all.

London, 2 Nov. 1949

This is the sort of English up with which I will not put.

Gowers, *Plain Words*

Nothing makes a man more reverent than a library.

Thoughts and Adventures

There is a good saying to the effect that when a new book appears one should read an old one. As an author I would not recommend too strict an adherence to this saying.

Attrib.

Writing a book is not unlike building a house or planning a battle or painting a picture … The foundations have to be laid, the data assembled, and the premises must bear the weight of their conclusions. Ornaments or refinements may then be added.

My Early Life

Writing a book was an adventure. To begin with it was a toy, an amusement; then it became a mistress, and then a master, and then a tyrant.

London, 2 Nov. 1949

I write a book the way they built the Canadian Pacific Railway. First I lay the track from coast to coast, and after that I put in all the stations (the facts).

Brendon, *Winston Churchill*

[Of his novel *Savrola*] I have consistently urged my friends to abstain from reading it.

My Early Life

If it weren't for painting, I could not live; I could not bear the strain of things.

Marchant, *Winston Spencer Churchill*

[Painting is] a wonderful new world of thought and craft, a sunlit garden gleaming with light and colour … an unceasing journey of entrancing discovery.

Thoughts and Adventures

Painting is complete as a distraction. I know of nothing which, without exhausting the body, more entirely absorbs the mind. *Ibid*

Painting is a companion with whom one may hope to walk a great part of life's journey. *Ibid*

Trying to paint a picture is like trying to fight a battle. It is, if anything, more exciting than fighting it successfully. But the principle is the same. It is the same kind of problem as unfolding a long, sustained, interlocked argument. *Ibid*

Happy are the painters, for they shall not be lonely.
Light and colour, peace and hope, will keep them
company to the end, or almost to the end, of the day.

Ibid

I cannot pretend to feel impartial about the colours. I
rejoice with the brilliant ones, and am genuinely sorry
for the poor browns.

Ibid

When I get to heaven I mean to spend a considerable
portion of my first million years in painting, and so get
to the bottom of the subject.

Ibid

Now I am learning to like painting even on dull days.
But in my hot youth I demanded sunshine.

Ibid

Maxims

It is a good thing for an uneducated man to read books of quotations.

My Early Life

There are two kinds of success – initial and ultimate.

House of Commons, 24 Feb. 1903

When you feel you cannot continue in your position for another minute, and all that is in human power has been done, that is the moment when the enemy is most exhausted, and when one step forward will give you the fruits of the struggle you have borne.

House of Commons, 3 March 1910

Honours should go where death and danger go.

House of Commons, 24 July 1916

You must look at facts because they look at you.

House of Commons, 7 May 1925

It is one thing to feel confident and it is another to impart that confidence to people who do not like your plan, and who feel the same confidence in their knowledge as you do in yours.

House of Commons, 10 June 1925

There never will be enough of everything while the world goes on. The more that is given the more there will be needed. That is why life is so interesting.

House of Commons, 16 June 1926

All wisdom is not new wisdom.

House of Commons, 5 Oct. 1938

An appeaser is one who feeds a crocodile hoping it will eat him last.

House of Commons, Jan. 1940

No idea is so outlandish that it should not be considered with a searching, but at the same time with a steady, eye.
House of Commons, 23 May 1940

Men may make mistakes, and learn from their mistakes … Men may have bad luck, and their luck may change.
House of Commons, 2 July 1942

The empires of the future are empires of the mind.
Harvard, Aug. 1943

There is no finer investment for any community than putting milk into babies.
Broadcast, 21 March 1943

A medal glitters; but it also casts a shadow.
House of Commons, 22 March 1944

It is a mistake to look too far ahead. Only one link in the chain of destiny can be handled at a time.
House of Commons, 1945

We must try to share blessings and not miseries.
House of Commons, 16 Aug. 1945

All the greatest things are simple, and many can be expressed in a single word: Freedom: Justice: Honour: Duty: Mercy: Hope.
Albert Hall, 14 May 1947

One ought to be just before one is generous.
Manchester, 6 Dec. 1947

You don't want to knock a man down except to pick him up in a better frame of mind.
New York, 25 March 1949

Perfect solutions of our difficulties are not to be looked for in an imperfect world.
Sheffield, 17 April 1951

Evils can be created much quicker than they can be cured.

Liverpool, 2 Oct. 1951

The true guide of life is to do what is right.

Huddersfield, 15 Oct. 1951

It is an error to believe that the world began when any particular party or statesman got into office. It has all been going on quite a long time.

Guildhall Speech, 9 Nov. 1951

Everyone has his day and some days last longer than others.

House of Commons, Jan. 1952

To jaw-jaw is better than to war-war.

Washington, 26 June 1954

Life is a perpetual holiday.

Brendon, *Winston Churchill*

The message of the sunset is sadness; the message of the dawn is hope.

My Early Life

It is the brightest hours that flash away the fastest.

Great Contemporaries

Nothing in this life is so exhilarating as being shot at without result.

My Early Life

Life is a whole, and luck is a whole, and no part of them can be separated from the rest.

Ibid

After all, a man's Life must be nailed to a cross either of Thought or Action. Without work there is no play.

Ibid

Chance, Fortune, Luck, Destiny, Fate, Providence seem to me only different ways of expressing the same thing, to wit, that a man's own contribution to his life story is continually dominated by an external superior power.

Thoughts and Adventures

There is an end to everything, and happily nothing fades as quickly as the memory of physical pain.

My Early Life

In one respect a cavalry charge is very like ordinary life. So long as you are all right, firmly in your saddle, your horse in hand, and well armed, lots of enemies will give you a wide berth.

Ibid

It is no use doing what you like; you have to like what you do ... human beings may be divided into three classes; those who are toiled to death, those who are worried to death, and those who are bored to death.

Thoughts and Adventures

Small people, casual remarks, and little things very often shape our lives more powerfully than the deliberate, solemn advice of great people at critical moments.

Ibid

It is hard, if not impossible, to snub a beautiful woman – they remain beautiful and the rebuke recoils.

Savrola

How little we foresee the consequences either of wise or unwise action, of virtue or of malice. Without this measureless and perpetual uncertainty the drama of human life would be destroyed.

The Second World War, vol. 1

It is impossible to quell the inward excitement which comes from a prolonged balancing of terrible things.

Stansky, *Churchill*

Ideas acquire a momentum of their own. The stimulus of a vast concentration of public support is almost irresistible in its potency. *Thoughts and Adventures*

Secrecy is not to be measured in altitude. If it were so, many might think that 'Bottom Secret' would be more forceful and suggestive. Brendon, *Winston Churchill*

If we look back on our past life we shall see that one of its most usual experiences is that we have been helped by our mistakes and injured by our most sagacious decisions.

Thoughts and Adventures

In sport, in courage, and in the sight of Heaven, all men meet on equal terms.

The Malakand Field Force

I know of no case where a man added to his dignity by standing on it.

Attrib.

Odd things animals. All dogs look up to you. All cats look down to you. Only a pig looks at you as an equal.

Attrib.

Saving is a very fine thing. Especially when your parents have done it for you.

Attrib.

A bullet in the leg will make a brave man a coward. A blow on the head will make a wise man a fool. Indeed, I have read that a sufficiency of absinthe can make a good man a knave. The triumph of mind over matter does not seem to be quite complete as yet.

The Malakand Field Force

Change is the master key. A man can wear out a particular part of his mind by continually using it and tiring it, just in the same way as he can wear out the elbows of his coat.

Thoughts and Adventures

Out of intense complexities intense simplicities emerge.
The World Crisis

It is a fine thing to be honest, but it is also very important to be right.
Comment on Stanley Baldwin

Go into the sunshine and be happy with what you see.
Thoughts and Adventures

It often happens that, when men are convinced they have to die, a desire to bear themselves well and to leave life's stage with dignity conquers all other sensations.
Savrola

In war: resolution
In defeat: defiance
In victory: magnanimity
In peace: goodwill.
The Second World War, 'Moral of the Work'

I have always laid down the doctrine that the redress of the grievances of the vanquished should precede the disarmament of the victors.
Great Contemporaries

Repartee

[Reply to Lord Curzon's comment that 'All civilisation has been the work of aristocracies'] It would be much more true to say, 'The upkeep of aristocracies has been the hard work of all civilisations.'

The People's Rights

Bessie Braddock: 'Winston, you're drunk.'
Churchill: 'Bessie, you're ugly. But tomorrow I shall be sober'.

Attrib.

Lady Astor MP: 'If you were my husband I'd poison your coffee.'
Churchill: 'If you were my wife, I'd drink it.'

Blenheim Palace, 1912

We have all heard how Dr Guillotine was executed by the instrument he invented ...[Sir H. Samuel: He was not.] Well, he ought to have been.

House of Commons, 29 April 1931

Don't talk to me about naval tradition. It's nothing but rum, sodomy and the lash.

Gretton, *Former Naval Person*

What! Give him [an MP] a peerage? Well, perhaps, provided it's a disappearage. House of Commons, 1954

[To de Gaulle]: Si vous m'obstaclerez, je vous liquiderai.

Brendon, *Winston Churchill*

[Reply to Aneurin Bevan] I should think it hardly possible to state the opposite of the truth with more precision. House of Commons

[Agreeing that Attlee was modest] Absolutely true. But then he does have a lot to be modest about. Attrib.

ny desire to be relieved of my
vanted was a compliance with my
e discussion.

The Second World War, vol. 5

policy is blinded by the passion of
ruggle with the enemy is over.
struggle with oneself. That is the

Thoughts and Adventures

utterflies ... The butterfly is the
ring, settling for an instant with
he sun, then vanishing in the

My Early Life

-speaking union.

Attrib.

words and vulgar fractions.

Margate, 10 Oct. 1953

deal to achieve nothing in the

ah Churchill, *A Thread in the Tapestry*

Maker. Whether my Maker is
ordeal of meeting me is another

Brendon, *Winston Churchill*

On Himself

I have derived continued benefit from criticism at all
periods of my life, and I do not remember any time
when I was ever short of it.

27 Nov. 1914

I have a tendency against which I should, perhaps, be on
my guard, to swim against the stream.

Accepting the leadership of the Conservative Party, Oct. 1940

I do not resent criticism, even when, for the sake of
emphasis, it parts for the time with reality.

House of Commons, 22 Jan. 1941

I am a child of the House of Commons. I was brought up
in my father's house to believe in democracy. 'Trust the
people' was his message. US Congress, Dec. 1941

I am certainly not one of those who need to be prodded.
In fact, if anything, I am a prod.

House of Commons, 11 Nov. 1942

Be on your guard! I am going to speak in French – a
formidable undertaking and one which will put great
demands upon your friendship for Great Britain.

Paris, after the Liberation of France, 1944

I have no intention of passing my remaining years in
explaining or withdrawing anything I have said in the
past, still less in apologising for it.

House of Commons, 21 April 1944

When I am abroad I always make a rule never to criticise
or attack the Government of my country. I make up for
lost time when I come home.

House of Commons, 18 April 1947

I have been a journalist and half my lifetime I have earned my living by selling words and I hope thoughts.
Ottawa, 12 Jan. 1952

It is no part of my case that I am always right.
House of Commons, 21 May 1952

Personally I am always ready to learn, although I do not always like being taught.
House of Commons, 4 Nov. 1952

I realised [upon attending a party given by the Prince of Wales in 1896] that I must be upon my best behaviour: punctual, subdued, reserved, in short display all the qualities with which I am least endowed.
My Early Life

I had no idea [in 1894] of the enormous and unquestionably helpful part that humbug plays in the social life of great peoples dwelling in a state of democratic freedom.
Ibid

Looking back with after-knowledge and increasing years, I seem to have been too ready to undertake tasks which were hazardous or even forlorn.
The World Crisis

I may claim myself to have added the words 'seaplane' and 'flight' (of aeroplanes) to the dictionary.
Thoughts and Adventures

I found that I could add nearly two hours to my working day by going to bed for an hour after luncheon.
My Early Life

There is no such thing as a negative virtue. If I have been of service to my fellow men, it has never been by self-repression but always by self-expression.
Marchant, *Winston Spencer Churchill*